Starting a Praise Band

Abingdon Press & The Church of the Resurrection
Ministry Guides

Starting a Praise Band

Lance Winkler
Adam Hamilton, Series Editor

ABINGDON PRESS
Nashville

STARTING A PRAISE BAND

This book is printed on acid-free paper.

Library of Congress Cataloging-in-Publication Data

Winkler, Lance, 1959-
    Starting a praise band / Lance Winkler.
        p. cm. — (Abingdon Press & the Church of the Resurrection ministry guides)
    ISBN 978-0-687-64594-7 (pbk. : alk. paper)
    1. Contemporary Christian music—Instruction and study. 2. Church music—Instruction and study. I. Title.

    MT88.W56 2007
    264'.2—dc22

                                                                    2007027158

07 08 09 10 11 12 13 14 15 16—10 9 8 7 6 5 4 3 2 1
MANUFACTURED IN THE UNITED STATES OF AMERICA

Contents

Foreword

At Church of the Resurrection both "traditional" and "contemporary" forms of worship are valued and important. I am reminded, when I think of contemporary Christian worship music, of the most prolific contemporary Christian music lyricist of all time. He composed over six thousand songs of praise that helped a new generation of Christians to worship with passion. His songs were to be memorized and sung "lustily." His name, as you have no doubt guessed, was Charles Wesley.

In this ministry guide Lance Winkler, a modern-day Charles Wesley, offers concrete and practical advice for how to start a contemporary worship service in any size church. Lance's music has touched thousands of people, and the words to his original songs have helped many to have their "hearts strangely warmed." He is passionate about music and even more passionate about worship.

Our hope is that this ministry guide will help you as you consider offering what may be a new form of worship for your congregation. Traditional worship and contemporary worship are both important forms of worship. Lance Winkler offers sage advice on how to embrace and embark on offering excellent contemporary worship for your church.

* *

At The Church of the Resurrection, we live daily with the goal to help people become deeply committed Christians. More than nominally religious. More than the Sunday pew holder. More than the spectator. We know these same people become more by doing more. We begin with the knowledge that people want the church to be theirs. They want to know God has a place for them. With that in mind, we recognized from the very start that specialized ministries utilizing the skills and talents of laypeople are fundamental to church life.

A church on the move will have specialized ministries capitalizing on the skills and talents of laypeople. They are your keys to succeed.

In developing these guides, we listened to the requests of smaller churches for practical resources to enlist laypeople for this purpose. These economical guides, written by proven leaders at our church, will serve as essential resources for innovative, creative, and, more than likely, nontraditional church workers who have little or no budget to work with. With these guides in hand, your laypeople will be ready to plunge into the work with excitement and courage instead of tentatively approaching it on tiptoe.

At the core of these guides is the belief that anything is possible. It's a challenge, but it's a truth. God can and does use us all—with that conviction we bring hope to the world.

—Adam Hamilton
Senior Pastor
The Church of the Resurrection
Leawood, Kansas

Begin at the Beginning

It was only a matter of time—from electricity came amplification, from amplification came a whole new collection of instruments that could be used as accompaniment in large settings. Take, for instance, the guitar. Where once this instrument was relegated to being strolled through restaurants and occasionally accompanying only the slightest of voices in a parlor, now it thundered through a hall, competing easily with cymbals and drums. Where once it took an entire orchestra to fill a large theater with sound, now you could plug in four longhaired lads and drown out an entire stadium full of screaming females. Almost.

Amplification didn't just transform instruments, it made a huge difference in public singing. Before microphones, to be heard in a large setting, your lungs, diaphragm, and vocal chords needed to cooperate efficiently. Vocal production was science/art. Now with 100,000 watts behind them, a crowd of thousands could hear the singer draw a breath (or hear Bob Dylan mumble).

So Thomas Edison is to blame for sparking a quantum leap of evolution in the world of music. What resulted was an entity known as the "Rock Band"—a configuration of trap set percussion, electric guitar, bass guitar, and give or take electric rhythm guitar and/or keyboard/s. This creature is also known as the **"basic rhythm section"** and has been the standard accompaniment for 99 percent of American music that has been heard on the radio for the last fifty years.

So how did the proverbial nose of the contemporary camel get in the door of the tent of tabernacle?

Let's be honest, this whole thing really started when we let those darn kids run the services on Sunday night every couple of months. We called them youth nights and back then it was kind of cute and endearing. Problem is, those kids grew up, started writing the checks, and turned into us. Nondenominational churches, using mostly contemporary music, grew and mainline church took notice of this new style of worship music that promised a more emotive atmosphere in which to experience the presence of God.

Why Contemporary Music and Why a Praise Band?

In the beginning of rock and roll music, the connotation of its very name was enough for the church to rightly keep it outside the sanctuary. However, no matter how lowly or deplorable its beginnings, given time, the stigma surrounding any style of music many times will fade. This is, of course, not a new phenomenon. Martin Luther, as a major part of the Reformation, changed the music of the church when he promoted chorale rather than contrapuntal-style singing. He used music to teach doctrine and theology rather than using it simply as an ornament of a Latin mass. In his time this was scandalous, and yet today chorale singing is the style of our traditional hymns.

Tradition is very powerful and will fight against any innovation—and it's likely there will be people who won't want anything but traditional music. One of my favorite Bible stories about the power of tradition is the account of Peter's response to the vision where he was told to eat unclean food.

"Surely not, Lord" (Acts 10:13 [NIV]). Consider the irony of those three words.

A change can be opportunity

We may be able to understand why Martin Luther changed the style of music in his day, but why do we need to change the style of music in our churches? What can contemporary praise music bring to our congregations that is different and useful? Besides just simply being more relevant, it offers a more emotive and experiential opportunity for the congregant.

• Studies have been done that show the music we are exposed to in our emotionally formative years is likely the style of music that will most speak to us for the rest of our lives. Think about the "our song" phenomenon. When two people are creating a powerful emotional bond with each other, a particular song with its lyric, melody, harmony, and groove can come to embody that emotion. This is where the band or rhythm section comes in. For 90 percent of us in today's culture it was that ensemble that created the soundtrack of our youth. It is a sound that people emotionally relate to, so using it as a vehicle to carry the gospel is only natural.

• Contemporary praise music is intentionally written to be less cerebral and more emotive. It is "praise and worship," not doctrinal and theological, as many of our hymns are. Certain emotive lines are repeated to allow a single concept to "sink in" and give the worshiper the opportunity to feel and experience the concept rather than just mentally assenting to it.

- Contemporary music's improvisational nature can give it more of an authentic feel. As an example, think of another worship expression that happens corporately—prayer. An improvisational prayer may seem more authentic than if someone stands and reads a prayer from two hundred years ago, even though the written prayer's grammar, words, and depth may be more powerful. And, that type of authenticity is valuable in today's culture.

The move to more contemporary music is truly inevitable, and now that the cat and genie are both out of their respective domiciles, there is no going back unless the electric power grids go down. So take a deep breath and exhale a prayer. I guarantee, God knows best, and the church is going to move forward.

CHAPTER TWO

How to Begin

The old folk tale "The Emperor's New Clothes" has always fascinated me. It tells how the masses can be silenced from telling the truth, if that truth would be perceived as not politically correct or "uncool" in any way. In that same way, just because it might be "uncool" to criticize contemporary music doesn't mean we should hide our collective heads in the sand about some of the obvious hurdles we created when we brought modern electrified music into the church.

We've got to admit that in some churches, the result of attempting contemporary music is unfortunate—especially when it's compared to the competent, organized worship of a few decades ago. Here are a few of the comments I have heard and some firsthand observations.

1. Unprofessional behavior and too casual an approach to God.

2. A performance mentality.

3. Too much—talk between songs, dependence on the musicians, repetition.

4. Music that is too loud.

5. Endless addition of new songs.

6. Technical glitches galore.

Ouch! But before we give up, let's step back and take a bit broader view of the situation. Traditional music has been used, honed, and codified for the last five hundred years. Only for the last decade or so have many churches been attempting to move into the arena of modern music. It is no wonder contemporary music, or the "Praise Band," has yet to find its feet.

So these things are mentioned not to frighten, but to remind us. There is a change going on. Change is hard, and part of the problem is that this change is harder than most of us think. The skills, preparation, execution, and even purposes of contemporary music are quite a bit different from that of traditional. We need to keep this in mind as we approach this transition and not underestimate it in any way.

Practical Steps

Some like lists—for those we've provided some numbers to go by. Of course, there may be all kinds of paths leading off of the numbered path, but these will give you an idea of getting started.

⊳ 1. **Pray.** This is not an obligatory suggestion on my part. You need to be convinced that this is what God wants for God's body, and if you want to know what God wants you need to ask. I can tell you with absolute assurance, you are going to need God's help. I have prayed many instrumentalists into place and myself through many difficult situations. Of all the tools you have to make this ministry a success, prayer is your most powerful.

⊳ 2. **Have** an overall vision for what you think God wants.

- When would the service take place? Is it contemporary music added to an existing service? Is it a whole new service Sunday or Tuesday or Saturday?

- What type of contemporary music do you want? Intergenerational, next generational? Piano driven, guitar driven?

▷ 3. **Make** sure your pastor suggested this endeavor or is fully on board. Pastors are the true worship leaders for your church. Present your vision to them. Be prepared to modify or radically change your vision. Realize going in that for various reasons, this may not be the season for your church to begin this ministry. Do not move forward unless your pastor is in agreement. This is a spiritual as well as practical admonition.

▷ 4. **Do** your homework up front. "For which of you, intending to build a tower, does not first sit down and estimate the cost, to see whether he has enough to complete it" (Luke 14:28). You may want to have some of this information put together before you even speak to the pastor. Your pastor needs to be aware of, and comfortable with, this information before moving forward.

- Put together a list of names you would want to contact to offer an opportunity for participation in this ministry. Don't solicit names yet. Notice I said, "offer an opportunity." Be careful not to paint yourself into a corner. You may think a person would have the skills for this, but upon further inspection discover they don't. Proceed with caution. Also gather names of those that you might think would support the ministry in various ways other than musically.

- Put together a list of equipment that may be needed—both sound and instruments. Get ballpark costs. Most musicians will have their own instruments, but your church may want to provide amps, drum kit, and so forth. Obviously, the more the church supplies, the more control it has.

- Interview some of the churches in your area that have a contemporary music ministry and ask about the impact it has had.

▷ 5. **Present** the vision along with the information in no. 4 to the leadership of your church. Shoot for 100 percent agreement. That may not be possible, but it makes things much easier if there is. Let me quote a friend of mine about his contemporary music attempt: "We were never able to win the wars in the budget process. It was one thing to grant permission for another service to exist, it was quite another to pay for it."

▷ 6. **Find** a contemporary director. Before going any further, find the person to musically take the reigns. If you don't yet have this person, every decision that is made, is made without the most important opinion. Much of what is done may have to be undone at possibly great expense, and not just monetary.

▷ 7. **Present** to the congregation. Make sure the pastor has a good presentation prepared. If he or she can do a sermon or series of sermons on worship in conjunction with the announcement, that's even better. Have other church leaders in support.

▷ 8. **Start** recruiting. Hold assessments, aka auditions.

▷ 9. **Set** a realistic start date—depending on the success and in light of the information gathered in the previous steps.

- How soon can you have the equipment you need?
- What is the level of talent and how long will it take them to be ready?
- Determine what type of group you can field. This could be anything from just guitar and vocals to a full rhythm section. Set the start date far enough out that you can prepare at least eight weeks of songs.

⇨ 10. **Get** a rehearsal space (preferably where you will be playing) and rehearsal schedule set. Pick out your repertoire. Rehearse.

⇨ 11. **Minister** and be prepared to be a blessing.

And in doing all of these things, try to remember you have to enjoy what you're doing.

CHAPTER THREE

What Kind of Contemporary Service?

Here you might ask, "If this ministry guide is about praise bands, why are you dealing with types of contemporary services?" My answer is, "To put together the proper band, you need to know what type of service they will be ministering in."

Having a viable plan in place is important. I can't tell you how many times I have had the conversation where a pastor or a traditional music director will declare, "We've tried contemporary music at our church and it just doesn't work." I ask, "When did you hold the service?" "Saturday night at 6:00," they reply. "Did you provide 'Sunday' school?" "No, I said it was **Saturday** night." "Did you provide child care?" "No." "Did the senior pastor preach or attend the service?" "No." Finally after several more questions with the response of no, I then ask, "Did you turn on the lights?" Here they usually respond with a yes, and I conclude, "I guess you're right. Contemporary music doesn't work for you guys."

Okay, I stretched that a bit, but often we put our contemporary services in less than desirable situations and when they don't meet expectations we blame "contemporary music." This is very common. We struggle with it at The

Church of the Resurrection. For example, we have only one worship time on Saturday and Sunday night, which makes it difficult to get volunteers because they can't volunteer at a service and then immediately attend the next. As a result, we don't have full children's programming at our Saturday night service, and the demographic on Saturday night reflects it. To tell the truth, I don't have an answer for it. Just be careful not to saddle "contemporary music" with the success or failure of a service. Worship music plays a huge role in whether or not your plan succeeds, but it is by far not the only player.

Purpose Determines Type

The **purpose** of your service will determine the type of service. The **type of service** will determine the type of music. The **type of music** will determine the type of leader, musicians, and configuration of the band along with programming of the music.

Purpose of a service

- Have a brand new church?
- Running out of room, so you need to go to multiple services?
- Want to reach a wider audience?
- Want to provide more time options for worship?
- Want to attract younger congregants?
- Want to provide alternative worship (a service with other worship expressions besides sermon, prayer, music, and liturgy)?
- Starting youth or young adult worship?
- Want to give opportunity for contemporary musical gifts to be utilized?
- Have a combination of these things?

Type of service

- Morning service

- Evening service
- Weeknight service
- Youth or Young Adult service
- A service to attract the nonreligious and nominally religious
- A boomer service
- An existing service with contemporary music added
- Alternative worship service

Type of contemporary music

These styles do not have hard edges, and this is definitely not a comprehensive list. At The Church of the Resurrection in our contemporary boomer services we play a smattering of all of them. Samples of artists listed below can be heard on online music sources.

▷ Adult Contemporary

Instrumentation: Bass guitar, drums, electric guitar, and either acoustic guitar and/or keyboard-driven. (At Church of the Resurrection, this has been our typical Saturday and Sunday evening fare. We often add brass, strings, B3 organ, and percussion.)

Description: Came out of the Jesus movement. It is largely acoustic guitar-driven but can also be keyboard-driven, as in the case of Michael W. Smith. This genre is the broadest and can extend stylistically from Don Moen to Israel Houghton to Chris Tomlin. If arrangements and presentation are properly nuanced the same songs can appeal across the age spectrum.

Artists: Michael W Smith, Chris Tomlin, Hillsong, Paul Baloche, and more are added all the time.

▷ Edgy (Rock) Contemporary

Instrumentation: Bass guitar, drums, electric guitar. Many times there will be a second electric—and sometimes acoustic guitar. Rarely if ever keyboard-driven; however, keyboards can be used.

Description: Can use many of the same songs as adult contemporary but done in an edgier way. Edgier means more volume, more distortion guitar in the mix, straight ahead driving "rock" drums. The overall sound can be less "produced," more "garage band." The appearance is important—generally a twenty-something looking band.

Artists: David Crowder, Phil Wickham, Lincoln Brewster—a list growing rapidly.

▷ Urban

Instrumentation: Bass guitar, drums, Hammond B3 organ with Leslie cabinet, clean electric guitar, keyboards (brass and choir).

Description: This style originated in African American churches. This is more B3-driven (a type of organ with a Leslie cabinet). It uses bass guitar, drums, and lead guitar (mostly nondistorted or "clean") and incorporates brass extensively. It utilizes jazz harmonies and progressions. Vocally there is generally a lead vocal, but it makes great use of a choir, and often the choir can lead the worship. It has jazz and gospel roots.

Artists: Brooklyn Tabernacle, Christ Church (Nashville)

▷ Alternative

Instrumentation: Piano, keyboard, acoustic guitar, percussion, and so forth.

Description: Unplugged. Usually done in more intimate settings. Rarely is there a trap set in this style.

Artists: 100 Portraits, Shane and Shane. There is a CD set, "Enter the Worship Circle," in this style.

▷ Blended

Instrumentation: This can range from typical rhythm section to orchestra and choir—and can include both.

Description: The optimum would be a service that could utilize the best of both worlds but that is very difficult to do. Generally this is a fusion of styles.

Artists: Brentwood-Benson music, Word music, Clydesdale, Prestonwood Baptist, and others.

Tips

1. If you are starting a Sunday morning contemporary service or are adding worship songs to a traditional service, you might consider a keyboard- or piano-driven band. There can be certain expectations at a Sunday morning service specifically around Christmas and Easter that would require a keyboard to fulfill them. Our contemporary services are primarily in the evenings, but I bring in an organist at Christmas and Easter to provide traditional accompaniment for certain pieces.

2. Nonreligious and nominally religious: *At Church of the Resurrection we are aware that on a given weekend as much as 40 percent of the congregation may not have made a decision for Christ.*

Quality: Not that quality isn't always important, and we always do our best, but here quality is a must. The nonreligious are often looking for a reason to remain that way. Be as authentic as possible. Also, about 99 percent of the time they are not going to participate, which means they will be sitting or standing there listening. The music should be at least marginally, dare I say, entertaining.

Programming: Since the nonreligious are not likely to participate at first means that a prolonged worship set of which they do not feel a part is probably not the way to go. We generally do a three-worship song set that ranges from ten to fifteen minutes. We have a "word in song" or "special music" selection before the sermon and then offertory after the sermon. However, the nonreligious in the youth and young-adult age group are looking for something experiential and are likely to be okay with longer worship sets.

3. Contemporary worship music is less about engaging the head and more about engaging the heart. It is difficult to create an atmosphere in which that can take place within two or three songs. Therefore, the real power of contemporary worship is hard to realize in seeker settings.

4. Flexibility: Having a plan in place and knowing what direction you want to go is necessary, but flexibility is the key. I would tend to allow the biggest factor in choosing a style to be dependent on the person God supplies to lead—then, that leader should play to his or her strengths. Also the people you attract to a service might not be those whom you planned. So flexibility? Absolutely necessary.

The Importance of the Praise Leader

"Easy is hard" is an old saying that really applies when it comes to contemporary music. It takes a lot of effort to make playing in the band look effortless. This is important since the music needs to have a relaxed, improvisational feel for the sake of authenticity. We need to be rehearsed enough that people say, "I can do that. It doesn't look that hard." Some think that good worship leaders never practice but simply "flow with the Spirit." The truth is, it's easier to respond to the Spirit's direction if you are prepared musically. It's pretty discouraging when the band doesn't know the right chords or words to a song. If all we ever did was "flow" in worship, there would be many things to detract from the congregation's ability to worship from the heart.

This aspect of contemporary music can be frustrating. We want people to feel that the band is just jamming and having a good time; however, this can foster the idea that it doesn't take as many resources or require as much effort or attention as traditional music does. The more effort put into a traditional piece of music, generally the more intricate and difficult it sounds. Oftentimes it's the opposite for contemporary music.

The Need for a Leader

With many church praise bands, the number one thing often found lacking is not individual musicianship, repertoire, or amount of dedication/effort—what is generally missing is *true musical direction.*

Let's follow a little story about Bob. Bob is a contemporary music leader in a medium-sized church. He is a drummer and knows his way around the guitar. He can read chord charts fairly well and has put together a good worship band with a couple of vocalists. The church has hired him to be their resident musician, and he has done this successfully for a number of years. The church has grown, and one day he is approached by his pastor who informs him there are several people in the congregation who play instruments. There is a clarinet and saxophone player, two flutes, a couple of violinists, trumpets, and a trombone. There is also a pianist and a dozen or so people who have fairly good voices and like to sing. The pastor says in light of this he would like Bob, the contemporary music director, to start a traditional orchestra and a choir. Bob immediately buys a little book titled something like "Starting an Orchestra and Choir." He attends a conference on "Traditional Music." He then makes a call to a local church that has an orchestra and choir director and asks her where he should start. She tells him, "In 4/4 time, a quarter note gets one beat, a whole note gets four, and Every Good Boy Does Fine." Bob has no idea what she is talking about. Bob is in trouble!

POTENTIAL PITFALL

Bob is a good musician and successful at making music, but he doesn't have the requisite training or experience to start this kind of musical endeavor with confidence. Most traditionally trained musicians would agree that Bob is deficient in his knowledge and experience of orchestras and choirs. As proof, they can point to the fact that this kind of expertise is made available in colleges with several different levels of degrees. It is here that a misunderstanding has arisen. Because contemporary rhythm sections have not been legitimized in the same collegiate way, it is assumed the same amount of knowledge and experience isn't needed to execute them.

I will note here, however, if Bob were to find the right repertoire, learn a few basic beat patterns, and set up some rehearsals, he could probably make a respectable start and have some level of success. His fear is as much an obstacle as anything. For him to put a well-crafted musical product forward that is not just an attempt or novelty, but something that will add favorably to the service every week, it will take a considerable amount of effort on his part. The above story is not meant to suggest that basic musical knowledge about theory and notation is not necessary to be successful in contemporary music—it is, of course, important for almost any style of music. However, shortly after learning musical rudiments, the specific skills and talents needed to perform these two styles begin to diverge rapidly.

This story is unlikely, and it would be unusual for a contemporary music director to be asked to start a traditional orchestra and choir, but this is done, in varying degrees, to traditional music directors time and time again. Most people don't understand that there are fairly divergent and specific skills and talents that apply to these different types of music.

Wanted: contemporary director, preferably a professional

As you can see from the example given earlier, the requirements for a contemporary director may be much different from the traditional orchestra and choir director. For the praise band what is needed includes:

- Someone who knows contemporary music and who knows how to rehearse and arrange on the fly.

- Someone who has a grasp of the sonic capabilities of contemporary instruments and how to play them. (Methods classes are required college curriculum for anyone studying conducting.)
- Someone who can audition prospective musicians and put the appropriate players in the best possible position to succeed.

Finding a contemporary band director

A couple of years ago I was looking for an assistant contemporary music director and began to interview several candidates in their late twenties/early thirties. When I asked one of the early prospects where he learned his craft, he responded, "I played a lot of gigs along the West Coast." Since I had traveled and gigged extensively in "my day," I asked him what clubs he had played. He replied, "Oh I've never played clubs, I've only played in churches." That was when it dawned on me, finally, there are very good musicians learning their craft in much better environments than those I had the opportunity to learn in. This doesn't mean you should only look for someone who has learned his or her skills in the church—there are some very good converted musicians out there who will do a great job. What it does mean is that there are an increasing number of qualified candidates.

The art/craft of directing is best learned sitting under someone who is a good contemporary music director. Short of that, your director should have at least participated extensively in a successful band. Many musicians have learned their instrument well, but have limited experience in an ensemble setting. Just because a person has the chops (can play) doesn't mean he or she is ready to lead a band.

> ▷ **Call** local churches that have successful contemporary programs to see if they have a qualified person who would like an opportunity to lead. When

these requests come to me, most times I don't like it. If I have a musician or singer who is good enough to lead somewhere else, then usually they are an integral part of what I am doing at my church. So be aware of this when you ask. How's that for honesty! Also ask for them to keep feelers out for possibilities.

▷ **Post** on the bulletin boards at:
  • Local colleges
  • Music Stores
  • Recording studios
  • Musician's union
  • Local papers

▷ **Network** with all of the colleges, music stores, and so forth. Get names of prospective people and make sure you make contact. This takes effort, but networking is the best way to come up with candidates.

▷ **Find** someone locally to consult with. It's not unusual for contemporary directors to be asked to consult with churches when they are setting up a contemporary music ministry. I have helped interview prospective leaders and auditioned and worked with their musicians and sound techs.

▷ **Advertise** on the web. There are several job search sites that deal exclusively with contemporary music.

You may find "the person" in a few weeks. However, it can take months, so take this possibility into account. This is honestly the most important decision you make that will determine the success or failure of your endeavor.

Dual Leadership

I would like to mention here the possibility of dual leadership. It can present its own set of problems, of course, but it can also be the answer to a lot of difficulties. Finding a single person who embodies all the skills needed for this position would be like finding your organist/pianist, choir/orchestra director, arranger, and soloist all rolled into one. Throw in organizational, people, ministerial, and public speaking skills and you've got yourself a superhero. This is why splitting the responsibilities in two can make sense. There are probably a dozen places the division could fall, but the most logical is **band director** and **up front vocalist/worship leader**.

I am not going to delve into this dual dynamic deeply but will only say in terms of choosing songs and arranging song sets they will have to be very compatible. I would also mention here that just because the one up front may be more visible, and (if stereotypes run true to form) perhaps more outgoing or personable, do not underestimate the importance of the band director. Especially when it comes to remuneration.

Directing/Arranging

It's not just about making good music—it's about communication. Music is primarily an emotive medium, so think about where you want the congregation taken emotionally. If the song is supposed to elicit excitement, reflection, or a feeling of majesty, think of ways to arrange the song to best speak that. You want the right instruments in the right register playing the right notes with the right sound at the right time.

Try to create an ebb and flow to the worship set. At times the whole band can be rockin'; at others, the arrangement breaks down to just acoustic guitar or piano. Intentionally arrange and rehearse those changes in mood. As you practice, try to listen to each instrument to make sure it is supporting the overall purpose and vibe you want the music to serve.

Every musician has an individual style, individual strengths, and individual limitations. Every room has its "audiosyncrasies" (just coined a new word). The things you hear being played on that new worship CD won't translate to every environment with every type of player.

Note: Generally the music on the CD is not designed to be a live worship experience. Every song is arranged for its individual maximum impact. So, for the most part, just playing back-to-back songs with arrangements directly from a CD will not give you the ebb and flow needed for a good live worship set.

Copyright

Making recorded music and customized charts available to the musicians is an important aspect of learning the songs. Before ever getting to arranging and rehearsal, the director of contemporary music must have a good way to get the music to the musicians. In the past, getting material out to band members and vocalists could be costly and time consuming—not to mention illegal. The problem is, hearing the music is as important as having the score in a contemporary band. The band needs to come to rehearsal prepared, so that means they have to have their own recording of the song and written music. The obvious answer is to have copies made—that is, of course, the illegal part.

The Church of the Resurrection dealt with this problem by evolving into a password-protected website (which the church has developed). Band members and vocalists can log in and download the MP3 and their charts. (We also have a scheduling and e-mailing module as a part of this system.) To do this legally, it is necessary to obtain several different licenses: a mechanical license from the song publisher to download each song and a master license from the record label to download the sound recording of each song. While the church administrated this for ourselves for a period of time, we found researching, finding information, negotiating licenses, and calculating and paying royalties to be an overwhelming and confusing process, to say the least.

We now use a subscribed service called Church Copyright Administration (CCA). They research, negotiate, secure, and review licenses. It gives us an online ability to build and submit project orders for copyright clearances. The CCA provides online accounting and royalty payments. This service calculates license royalty rates, invoices the church for total royalty fees due, and makes payments to individual copyright owners on your behalf. If you pay quarterly royalties, CCA will not pay royalties on your behalf but will provide a royalty statement template for your use. CCA has a copyright administration staff with twenty-five plus years of professional experience. It's like online banking for copyright clearances.

The technology for how we receive and disseminate information seemingly changes daily. The legalities that try to protect intellectual property struggle to keep up, and convenient ways to adhere to the laws are even slower in developing, but things are beginning to come into focus. Good faith efforts to be in compliance with copyright laws are important not only as a testimony to the world but also as a way to help support creativity in the future. The church is the greatest creative organism in creation. Paying for the things we use in worship can funnel support for creativity back into Christ's kingdom. The blessing for God's people as we pay for things we use could result in the recapturing of the culture.

You as the Director

More than half of what the contemporary music director does is arrange, and much of that is done in rehearsal. This is, of course, how directing contemporary is quite different from directing traditional. Although both are crafting the overall sound of a group, the traditional music director is rarely rearranging the music. Consider what songs best fit together and in what order. Also what short, spoken statement might be made for the worshiper's benefit.

Be aware of your room acoustics and your congregation; don't try to take either of them where they are not ready to go. Choose and arrange the music for what is in the best interest of the service, the church, and consequently, the kingdom. Remember: It's not just about making good music, it's about communication.

When preparing music for worship, consider two very important points:

1. The world takes its music seriously. We are surrounded by high quality music. Everywhere we go, we hear professional music, whether it's in a restaurant, an elevator, in our own car, or in our living room. We grow up with an appreciation for well-performed music, and we play for people who know good music when they hear it.

2. How would you prepare if you were asked to play for a president, prime minister, or king of a nation? No doubt you would practice hard because you would want to get it right. We hold a reception for the King of kings once a week. We hold meetings to honor God and to further the kingdom in our lives and communities. We offer the best of everything we have, including our music. The quality of our music makes a statement that says, "Worshiping God is important to us, and we're going to work hard at sounding the best we can."

When, Where, and What

At The Church of the Resurrection, we prefer to rehearse in the same place we are going to play, which in our case is the main sanctuary. We practice Thursday evenings to have the rehearsal as close to the weekend as possible.

We will work on the coming weekend's music that usually consists of:
- Instrumental prelude
- Three praise songs

- Word in song (special music, usually with band and vocalists)
- Offertory (usually with band and vocalists, sometimes we introduce a new praise song here)
- Postlude (generally one of the earlier praise selections)
- Various musical transitions, stand and greet music, and so forth.

Band rehearsal starts at 6:30 p.m. At the same time, that week's scheduled mic singers—those who lead from the front of the stage—meet with our choir director in a separate rehearsal hall. At 7:00, our choir joins the mic singers and they rehearse together till 8:00. Then, depending on the selections for that week, the appropriate singers will join the band on the chancel and rehearse for another thirty plus minutes. Roughly a two-hour rehearsal.

The band works from charts and the choir from written music. We seldom teach the choir by rote. The band uses either lead sheets or measures with chords. We rarely use charts that have only words and chords.

We work the music according to a specific order, starting with the new and most difficult material. (Areas of possible difficulty have already been noted by the director.) We generally run through the "praise songs" last, paying attention to transitions. If there is a spoken transition we try to rehearse that also. We rarely work more than a week in advance on the music.

Rehearsal give and take

Most of the things said immediately following will be obvious from the recordings you are using, but here is a sample of instructions I give. This, of course, is in no way comprehensive, but it is a sense of what to listen for and the language used to communicate.

- Lead guitar: "Use a different color of chord like a minor nine chord instead of a straight minor, double the bass line with low single note distortion, arpeggiate a section rather than play rhythm, play 'power chords.' "

- Keyboard: "Play a low fat pad with open fifth or octaves, play more or less rhythmically in specific sections, use a seventh or ninth, use more open voicing . . ."
- Bass guitar: "Try a different groove, put the accent on a different beat, give me eighth notes, walk the bass in this section, play directly with the kick, play up the neck."
- Percussion: "More cow bell!" (just kidding)
- Drums: "Try a different kick or snare pattern, put a cymbal swell here, go to your ride cymbal, mute the crash, play full snare instead of side stick, have the band all drop out except for the drummer and vice versa . . ." Drums are, in my opinion, the most important instrument. Most of my instruction will go to them. To a great extent in performance the drummer is the bandleader.
- And my favorite instruction for all the instruments, "Don't play in this section!"

Rules to Direct By

When children learn to read, they must follow certain rules to help get them through a page. It is slow and painful and they find that all the rules don't always apply. There will come a time when they won't have to consciously think, "How does a long 'o' sound?" they will just read. The same is true with directing a band. The director will get better as time goes on and won't have to think about the rules—it will just come naturally. Until then, here are a few suggestions. They may seem slow and painful and all the rules don't always apply, but they can help you read a rehearsal.

1. **What makes this song this song?** Pushes, harmonies, guitar riffs, hooks, and so forth.

2. **The Groove.** Decide the musical purpose of the song. Should it push ahead? Should it "lay back" on the backside of the beat? Let the band groove on a short section of the song so the musicians won't worry about the chords and form and just listen to each other and concentrate on feel.

3. **Kick drum, snare drum, and bass player are the heartbeat of your music.** Everything else is built on this foundation. If you don't have the right feel, groove, or energy in your song, listen first to the kick and bass. If you try to add feel or energy with guitar, keyboard, or vocal, and the problem is really in the kick snare and bass, you will compound your problem.

4. **Right foot (of the drummer), Left hand (of the bass player).** This rule is, of course, another aspect of rule no. 3. Make sure the rhythm pattern of the bass is basically lining up with the rhythm pattern the kick drum is playing. On average worship songs, the patterns should generally be one to two measures long. This will tighten up your sound and give it punch and energy.

5. **The piano player's pinkie *(the left one to be exact)*.** God gave us that bass player for a reason—make sure the keyboard player's left hand isn't stepping all over them. Piano players usually learn to cover all the parts, but playing in an ensemble is a whole different game. There are moments when the bass notes of a piano add a creative element, but the bass notes should be thought of as a completely different instrument and added only when they make a specific aesthetic contribution.

6. **The 100 percent rule *(rhythmically)*.** There is a rhythm pie: if the piano player is eating up 50 percent of the rhythm then you can't have your rhythm guitar player and lead guitar player chowing down on the rest because your drummer goes hungry. Example: *If the drummer is playing a disco groove with 16ths on the hi-hat, the keyboard should be playing whole notes or what I call bell chords.*

7. **The 100 percent rule (*harmonically*).** Harmonically it's the same thing. If the piano is playing lush-colored chords have your guitar player arpeggiate or sometimes play a single note rhythmically. The 100 percent rules are really about playing complementary and not letting players get in each other's way. The acoustics of your room can play a part in this. For example, if you are in a room with a lot of natural reverb, many times an intricate bass guitar riff can be lost or sound out of time and tune. An intricate kick drum pattern can also be trouble in the same conditions. The music will be better served if more simple and tight playing (see rule no. 2) is observed. Your players will not like it if you tell them this, especially if the riff or pattern is really cool.

8. **Less is more.** Get musicians used to not playing. Make sure that everything you are playing is necessary to the overall effect of the music.

9. **Tune.** If all of the guitar players don't use electronic tuners, invest in one for the church. Let's also mention drum tuning. Good drum heads and proper tuning are very important. There are instructional DVDs out there. NEW strings! No more need be said.

10. **Listen, listen, listen.** Go out into the pews and listen to what the congregation is hearing. This may be painful, but essential, and you will often discover that what's working on stage or in your headphones or what worked on the CD does not work in the house. The director should listen to how he or she gives direction. Listen to the musicians. Listen to comments from the congregation.

11. **Ask yourself, "Are the *'moments'* in the worship set and song there?"**

12. **Record services and/or rehearsals.**

13. **Always work on lowering stage volume.**

14. **Be honest with yourself about what you hear.**

Rehearsal hints

It's important to keep in mind that the band is made up of people who have invested many, many hours over many, many years learning to create on their instrument, so give them space to express themselves musically. In contemporary music most of what the musicians are playing they are creating since it isn't written down. This means they might be more personally invested in what they are playing than their traditional counterparts would be. When corrected, they can feel it pretty deeply. Also, traditional musicians grew up playing in orchestra and band settings, where they are used to receiving instructions. In the case of many contemporary instrument players they might have received very little instruction up to this time.

Don't be shy, make what you might think are drastic suggestions but do not get married to any idea. It's very difficult to tell good musicians that they have to change what they are playing. It can be intimidating, and it's tempting to let insecurity show by being too directive or demanding or being too timid and not saying what needs to be said.

The director must listen honestly and to a great extent dispassionately. Be careful not to get hung up on a specific "moment" or musical passage. The law of diminishing return is at work here. You don't want to spend 90 percent of your rehearsal working out 4 percent of one of the tunes.

Be flexible!

Nuts and Bolts

Since, as we discussed earlier, the contemporary praise band is the melding of music and technology, directors in this genre need to be conversant in both. We need to know not only how to play our keyboard but also a little about why it sounds the way it does. Many times I have rehearsed the band over and over because it didn't have the sound I wanted—only to discover it was an audio problem. Equally often it has been the other way around.

Granted, most musicians do not have a passion for technical issues, so it can prove to be tedious and, therefore, a challenge—though a necessary one. This chapter will provide some structural information for the person new to contemporary music and some reminders for the experienced.

Sound Engineer

This book is not the venue for an extensive study in acoustics or audio engineering; however, without proper sound reinforcement it doesn't matter what type of band you put together, so some discussion is necessary. How important is sound reinforcement to contemporary worship? Very! Making the music is only half; the other 50 percent is sound amplification.

Even if you are only putting vocals through it, you should always have someone near the mixing board. The more instruments you put into the FOH (front of house) system, the more you will be in need of someone who can aesthetically mix those instruments. This is not always the person who is the best at technical things or who has the greatest interest. Just because someone can hook the system up (which is not the easiest thing in the world) doesn't mean this is the person to run sound. Someone wouldn't come and play the piano just because he or she technically knows how the piano works and would like to try it. Make no mistake, mixing sound takes a level of God-given talent—this is more important to the overall sound than any one instrumentalist on stage.

Set expectations from the beginning—make this an auditioned position just like a vocalist or instrumentalist.

If you are the music director, for your own sanity and theirs, find someone you are compatible with, and someone you feel you can trust. Of all relationships specifically in this ministry, the music director/leader and sound engineer **is perhaps the most vital.**

Instruments

Good sound doesn't begin at the sound mixer, it starts on stage with the individual instruments and amps. A favorite saying of the computer world, "garbage in, garbage out," can also become the favorite saying of the sound person. That's why in this section we will talk not only about sound boards, microphones, and so forth, but also touch on the instruments themselves.

Drums

Because the drums are the most important instrument in the band, they require the most attention not only in rehearsal but also in the area of sound. Acoustically it is the loudest instrument in the rhythm section; therefore, it offers the greatest sonic challenge. The tone and volume of your drums can play a huge role in the success of your contemporary ministry. Make sure the drums fit the room and genre of music from the outset.

There are very few instances in a church setting where live drums do not need some kind of sound dampening. Generally you should start with an acrylic drum shield. Any store that sells drums will know where to purchase this item. Or, just check the Internet under drum shield. The amount you enclose the drums in can vary depending on your room size, acoustics, and what type of sound you want from the drums. For instance, our last sanctuary was a 1,600-seat room, but because of the acoustics on the chancel we had to construct a complete enclosure for the drums.

Costs can range from $400 to $2,000. There are a few instances when the drum set does not need some type of sound dampening. These occasions are rare and usually pretty specific and mostly have to do with edgier, less "produced" garage-band styles of music. We now do worship in a 3,200-seat sanctuary with decent acoustics and still use an acrylic shield in front with a sound trap behind. This is mostly to stop the drums from bleeding into other live mics on the stage.

Caution: Don't just be concerned with what's in front of the drums, but look at what's behind them. If you put the drums up against a hard reflective surface, it won't matter what kind of shield you put in front of them.

You will not stop all or maybe even most of the sound coming directly from the kit so don't try to achieve that. The drummer has to use some tactics and techniques to help in this regard. Different types of sticks can make a huge difference as can just softer playing. Both of these things affect the sound of the drums, and lighter playing can interfere with the drummer's timing. Finding the right balance for the drums in church requires patience with intention. If you have never used drums in worship before, they might take some getting used to.

Tuning the drums is also very important. There are many instructional books and DVDs out there for that. New and proper heads are very much like new strings for a guitar— they can help immensely. Remember, "garbage in, garbage out." If you amplify something that sounds bad, you will only make it louder. How's that for obvious.

Electronic drums

Okay, I prefer acoustic drums. I like the energy they create and the nuance they are capable of. However there are scenarios where electronic drums serve the purposes of the church better. This is for the obvious reasons—they can sound great and you can turn the volume up and down. They can be pricey, but are comparable to a kit with sound dampening.

We lost two very good drummers for the two years The Church of the Resurrection used electronic drums. They told me they would love to play in the band, but we didn't allow their instrument anymore. This is understandable . . . so be prepared if you go this direction.

Electric guitar

Place the electric guitar on the list of sound concerns. Part of what generates a distortion guitar's distinctive sound are the tubes and speaker of the amp itself. I prefer the warmth of tubes over solid state, so for this reason our lead guitar player is the only instrument with an amp on stage—but the amp is behind an acoustically treated wall with a blanket over it. Then we mic it and put it in the monitors and house.

You can run the guitar directly into the house and back through your monitors. You will miss out on the sound created by the amp and generally the guitar player won't care for this. If the guitar player is careful with the stage volume, an amp on stage should not be a problem. I have found that half of what are considered volume problems is usually a frequency problem (when a specific frequency is displeasing) or the types of sound being used (distortion instead of clean, etc.) or just how the instrument is being played or used in the arrangement. For electric guitar, learning to play the notes and chords is only part—as much time needs to be spent on getting the right sound out of your pedals and other outboard gear.

Note: use examples from recordings to challenge players to find the proper sounds for what you want to achieve.

Keyboard

This is less about sound and more about keyboard functionality. We mic up a large acoustic grand on stage, which creates its own set of problems. My suggestion is to use some form of synthesizer for your piano and other keyboard needs. Pro keyboards come in a number of sizes with various numbers of keys. It's common to find keyboards with 88, 76, 61, 49, 36, and even 25 keys. You will also hear the words "hammer action," "semi-weighted," and "synth action" in regard to keys. You must determine which combination of keybed action type and number of keys will provide the best combination of feel and functionality.

In a professional setting, the only issue of sound quality that can make a difference is the sample rate and bit depth of the samples, such as 24-bit/96kHz, which is rapidly becoming the standard. With many synthesizers offering sounds that were recorded in world-class studios with rare vintage gear, the question of sound quality becomes an issue of whether or not the sounds a particular synth produces inspire you.

The type of synthesizer you need depends on the type of music you want to make and also on what other sound sources you have. Do you want authentic analog modeling or clean sounding sample playback? If you want realism or plan to do orchestral, mainstream, or pop worship music, you will need convincing piano, string section, brass, and so forth, in which case a sample playback synth will work. If you are doing urban, alternative, or edgy worship, then an analog modeling synth could be more appropriate. If you have a keyboard-driven band, a dedicated synth for piano and a secondary keyboard for pad sounds, organ, strings, and brass, is what is most common.

- Knobs and controllers. The bare necessities are a functioning pitch wheel and mod wheel. Don't leave home without them. Make sure that the knobs and sliders transmit MIDI continuous controller messages. These become very useful as you find your way around the MIDI universe.
- RAM/ROM—Upgradeable. This is an important issue in choosing a keyboard. ROM expansion allows you to add sound cards, thus extending the sonic and useful life of your keyboard. For sampling keyboards, the amount of RAM determines how much sampling time you have.

Cost of Instruments

Okay, this saying is so old I don't even want to say it, but when it comes to instruments it is absolutely true: "You get what you pay for." The problem is there is such a wide range of prices. Take acoustic guitars. You can walk into an average music store and see them priced from $150 to $3,500. It's true that a good musician can make a cheap instrument sound good. (I used to gig with a keyboardist who played a $150 Casio. He played so well no one cared.) It's true that the most expensive guitar in the world won't make a good musician out of a bad one. And, dollars are no substitute for practice. That being said, you can really undermine your work with cheap gear.

This is the very lowest you should expect to spend. If you go any lower you will be affecting playability and sound in a negative way.

- Keyboard: expect to spend $800+
- Electronic drums, mesh heads: $1,500+
- Acoustic drums, cymbals, and hardware: $1,500+
- Electric guitar: $400+
- Acoustic guitar with electronics: $500+
- Bass guitar: $400+

Sound System Configurations

This is some very skeletal information that can start your conversation about sound reinforcement. It's always a good idea to bring in somebody who knows sound from the very beginning, but with more than 350 to 400 congregants, it really is a necessity.

The most basic of systems consists of a mixer, amp, microphone/s, and front-of-house speakers (speakers facing the congregation). Only vocals would run through this system. Others would use their individual amps for the FOH sound and their monitor.

On the other end of the spectrum you would have a FOH system with all the instruments mic'd or running direct through it: a separate monitoring system controlling in-ear or open monitors or a combination of the two, outboard effects and equalization.

I won't go into all the possible configurations in between the above two, but here are some possible benchmarks. I am going to list numbers of congregants and advise what instruments should be running through the FOH. I will assume the room size is 15 percent larger in correlation with the congregant number.

- Under 10-50, only vocals—*Basic sound system*
- 50-150, vocals and acoustic guitar—*Basic sound system with monitors*
- 150-350, vocals and acoustic guitar, keyboards, and percussion—*Basic sound system with monitors; at least 16-channel, preferably 24-channel board*
- By 350+ congregants, you should try to run everything, vocals, acoustic guitar, keyboards, percussion, lead guitar, bass guitar, and drums through FOH—*Basic sound system with monitors; at least 24-channel, preferably 32-channel board. You will need Subs for FOH to carry the kick drum and bass guitar.*

Volume levels: I won't give you decibel levels. Some say you should be able to hear the person next to you sing. I think you should be able to hear yourself sing and have trouble hearing your neighbor. For me the type of sound is more important than decibels. I listen for a full, warm, encompassing sound, a sound that envelops the listener but doesn't overwhelm or assault them. The sound should support and inspire the congregant to sing. There should not be any unpleasant frequencies or sounds that stick out. Listen for each instrument and voice to make sure nothing unpleasant is going on. This may seem all too obvious, but listening critically and being willing to take action is very important.

Sometimes this is a sound issue caused by sympathetic vibration according to the audio characteristics of a room. You can use a spectral analyzer to find these frequencies by analyzing white noise. You can then minimize those frequencies that are accentuated by the room and boost those that are absorbed by using a graphic equalizer across the system. This is called "ringing out" a room.

A Sound System's Individual Components

Here is a bit of information you can start with when you begin looking at systems. Again, this will only get you started.

Power amplifiers

- **Power.** Generally you should pick an amplifier that can deliver power equal to twice the speaker's continuous IEC power rating. This means that a speaker with a "nominal impedance" of 8 ohms and a continuous IEC power rating of 350 watts will require an amplifier that can produce 700 watts into an 8 ohm load. For a stereo pair of speakers, the amplifier should be rated at 700 watts per channel into 8 ohms.
- **Headroom.** A quality professional loudspeaker can handle transient peaks in excess of its rated power if the amplifier can deliver those peaks without distortion. Using an amp with some extra "headroom" will help assure that only clean, undistorted power gets to your speakers. Some professional amplifiers are designed so they have additional headroom. These amps can cleanly reproduce transient peaks that exceed the amplifier's rated power. In this case, select a model with an output power rating equal to the continuous IEC power rating of the speaker. Consult the amplifier manufacturer or owner's manual to learn more.
- **Budget.** If budget restraints or legacy equipment force you to use an amplifier with less power, extreme care should be taken to see that the amplifier is not driven into clipping. It may surprise you to learn that low power can result in damage to your speaker or system, not to mention ear fatigue caused by the resultant distortion.

Soundboards or mixers

- **Mic/line/instrument ins.** How many do you need? Don't forget to include direct inputs from keyboards, guitar and bass amps, and DJ stations. And keep future expansion in mind.

- **EQ.** How complete do you want to be? Some mixers offer basic low/high frequency adjustments; others provide multiband parametric EQ on each channel with high and low shelving.

- **Direct outs/inserts.** Do you need input channels to be routed to external effects or other processing gear?

- **Onboard or outboard effects.** If you are inserting a new mixer into your current rig with outboard effects gear you already own, you may not need built-in effects on your mixer. However, one appeal of onboard effects is that you don't need to transport so much of other gear to and from gigs.

- **How many buses.** This depends on your signal routing needs. If you're sending monitor mixes from your main mixer, you may need an 8-bus mixer to handle band members' different monitoring demands.

- **Mono or stereo mains.** Your output configuration depends on your combination of amplifiers and speakers.

- **Monitor outs.** Again, you need to decide how your monitoring environment will be run. Choices range from "none" all the way to a separate monitor mixer onstage that receives the same inputs your main mixer does.

- **Powered or unpowered.** In most cases, powered mixers are designed for smaller groups and smaller venues where speed of setup and convenience are of primary concern. Bigger, more complex systems generally use either powered speakers or separate power amps.

FOH loudspeakers

Big, small, or in between? Without getting into the math of room volume in cubic feet to speaker size/numbers, you can quickly narrow down your list by recognizing that a small room doesn't need multiple speaker cabinets to carry a voice and guitar. Conversely, a 1,000-seat sanctuary needs the power and air-moving ability that only multiple pairs of 15-inch woofers and high-powered HF transducers can fill.

- How many (sets of) speakers do you need? Again, this depends on your venue. If it is a 200-seat sanctuary that demands significant volume levels, you might be best served by a pair of column-type speakers, one standing on either side of the stage. If you have more real estate to cover you could use a quartet of two-way powered speakers, such as JBL's EON series. You could add a subwoofer like the JBL MP255S to a set of stand-mounted two ways to effectively cover both a larger space and the full frequency range.

- Powered or unpowered? This is a great question to ask. **Powered speakers can solve a multitude of issues.** Remember that powered speakers require access to extra electrical outlets.

- How much power do you need? See the Power Amplifiers section. Contrary to popular belief, you're more likely to damage your speakers with an underpowered amp than with one that has too much power, so don't scrimp here.

- Do you need a subwoofer? A subwoofer can significantly increase the low-frequency capability of your system. It can also help "clean up" your sound by taking some of the low-frequency load—and the accompanying distortion—away from your other speakers, which can actually let you run at lower volume levels while still maintaining the "punch" of your performance.

- Do you want your speakers floor-based or stand-mounted? Can you "fly" your speakers? Many speaker models have hanging points for ceiling or wall mounting.

Microphones

When choosing a mic for live performance, consider a number of factors. Naturally, good sound quality goes without saying, but there are other equally important factors as well:

1. The mic should be rugged and reliable in order to hold up to the rigors of nightly live performance and travel.
2. It should be comfortable and easy to hold while performing.
3. It should have good resistance to feedback.
4. It should be able to handle high SPL (sound pressure levels).

Of the characteristics mentioned above, the mic's ability to resist feedback requires a little more in-depth discussion. Resistance to feedback is where the mic's polar pattern comes into play. The polar pattern determines the "listening area" of the mic. A cardioid or super-cardioid pattern tends to be more directional, picking up sounds from in front of the mic and rejecting sounds from behind (such as stage noise from monitors, amps, and so forth). This will typically increase gain before feedback, which makes either pattern more desirable for live use. One mic with good sound and incredible gain before feedback is the Sure Beta 57A.

Generally, the mic of choice for stage has been dynamic mics like the Sure SM58 because they're rugged and can handle high SPLs (and eager volunteers) since the diaphragm is more rigid than that of a condenser mic. The trade-off is less response to transients resulting in a less detailed sound than in studio condenser vocal mics. Hoping to combine the best of both worlds by offering studio-quality sound in a hand-held stage mic, a number of manufacturers have introduced a new generation of condenser mics.

Wireless microphones

At Church of the Resurrection, we use wireless mics almost exclusively. They afford a lot of freedom on the stage. However, the signal is compressed so it can be transmitted, and for that reason I prefer the sound of a "wired mic." They can be quite pricey.

Monitors

At The Church of the Resurrection, we use a combination of in-ear and wedge monitors. The band uses an analogue Furman system where each player has control over his or her mix. There are digital personal monitoring systems out there—Aviom is a big name in that arena. At the piano I have a powered wedge so I can use the Furman to control my own mix.

I really recommend the personal monitoring systems. It can remedy a lot of issues, time spent on the monitor mix, quality of that mix, stage volume, and so forth. Of course, the flip side is, in-ear monitoring can give you a feeling of isolation and you can lose that sense of ensemble playing. It took a fair amount of time to transition to this type of monitoring, but in the end it has been worth it at The Church of the Resurrection. (However, we do play on wedges every chance we get.)

So despite the recent buzz about in-ear monitors, ultimately, there is no one tool that renders others obsolete. Just as a musician's physiology determines instrument choice and playing comfort, personal preference and need are factors in determining whether a wedge, side fill, stand-mounted monitor, or in-ear monitor is right for your situation.

For example:

- Backup singers who need to hear themselves clearly as well as the rest of the chorus would find it invaluable to have in-ear monitoring for staying on pitch and blending with the other vocalists.
- A drummer and bass player's performance would benefit from hearing and feeling the beat pumping on stage.
- Keyboard/synth players might benefit from a stand-mounted monitor to hear themselves cut through the mix.
- An acoustic pianist or other acoustic musicians whose instruments play in a lower or wider spectrum will benefit from a larger full-range speaker.

The goal is to find the right monitor system that is best suited to your individual playing mixer.

CHAPTER SEVEN

Spiritual Aspects of the Band

"This is not a performance." "This is for God's glory, not ours." "We need to disappear." "People's attention should be on Christ, not on us." No matter how often they are said, they don't become any less true. We need to be constantly reminded to check the motives behind what we do, much like how the Israelites were told to always keep the words of the Scriptures right before their eyes. So what is it that gets in the way? Let's all say what *"the problem"* is together . . .

Everybody wants to be a rock star!

Again, electricity played a role as the catalyst for this circumstance. Amplification and recording technologies have broadened possible audiences exponentially. In the past, minstrels were noticed, but they weren't the icons of society they are today. In some recent surveys, the top occupations rated among our youth are not firefighters or police officers, but professional athletes and musicians. Popularity has been around forever, but mass media has created the phenomenon of "The Star," and that type of persona can creep into the church.

Some might say, "See, here is another reason why contemporary music should not be a part of worship." But let's be honest, **everybody** has *"the problem."* All of us want to be noticed; all of us like it when the world revolves around us. It is the very human condition we call pride. It infuses and motivates everything we do. Differing activities give people a greater or lesser chance to display *"the problem."* For instance we don't think about pride being a problem with most occupations, but we can spot a church diva in an instant. There is a difference, of course, and that is in the case of ministry the stakes are high. ***The attitude in which the band and singers take the pulpit is very important.***

Public Worship

Let's take a positive approach to this. Since contemporary music seems to be an activity that gives people the chance to display *"the problem,"* instead of viewing it as contemporary music creating a difficulty for us, view it as an opportunity for personal growth. *When impatience, perfectionism, frustration, negativity, anxiety, nervousness, anger, ego, paranoia, pride, and so on begin to creep up in leading worship, it's a signal to* **reevaluate, repent,** *and* **relax.** Pray ahead of time that the Holy Spirit will prompt you to **reevaluate** (remember what it's all about)**, repent** (for making this "about me"), and **relax** (it's just healthier).

Living into this is more difficult than just hearing and agreeing with it. When the worship team is about to take its place in front of the church and things don't seem to be lining up right and on top of it all you are about to sing and your throat is sore, then remember that **this isn't about me**. (It's also hard to remember **it's not about me** when things are going exceptionally well.)

Remember that God is more interested in *who* is worshiping than in *how* the person is worshiping. It is important that the worship leaders be gifted in their various musical areas, but our Lord is more about what the worship is doing to the worshiper inside than how it sounds outside. Let's face it.

God is not in need of talent—there are some pretty good voices singing around the throne at this very moment.

Negative attitudes

However, let's drill down into the issue a little more. In many artists, negative attitudes seem to be defense mechanisms to protect against **insecurity**. In some cases, simple words of encouragement (Eph. 4:29) can be helpful. These words can prove very difficult to give because this defense mechanism will often elicit the opposite of words of encouragement. Most often, however, insecurity results not from lack of self-esteem, but from lack of faith. People try to manufacture their own security, which negates the need for faith.

Here are the concepts needed: "If God has called us to this ministry, God will tell us, and if God calls, God will equip." And, "Any ability you have is a gift not to or for you, but to and for the building up of the kingdom of God." These things are fundamental to our Christian faith but need to be kept right before our eyes so we can maintain purity in our motives. This type of faith removes "the problem" of **Everybody wants to be a rock star!** Of course, all this doesn't only apply when leading worship, but applies to all aspects of life.

When contemporary music creates a scenario where ego can be a potential problem, it's actually giving us an opportunity for personal growth and obedience. For me it creates a situation where my shortcomings are accentuated. In another line of work I don't know that I could have identified them so readily and have the chance I've had to really concentrate on them.

Conflict

There might not be another relationship with greater volatility than that of those involved in the church praise band. Asking individuals who have spent years practicing their individual instruments to meld creatively is a dangerous formula, but fold in artistic temperament, mix with liberal amounts of religion, and then turn up the heat of performing every week and you have quite a recipe. So, it's not, **if** you have conflict, but **when** you have conflict.

When you do, look to this: "Therefore, if you are offering your gift at the altar and there remember that your brother (or sister) has something against you, leave your gift there in front of the altar. First go and be reconciled to your brother (or sister); then come and offer your gift" (Matt. 5:23-24). As worshipers, we are offering our gift at the altar: God is requiring us to have clean relationships if we are serving God. Notice also that we are to be proactive in this, not just reactive. You are responsible to go, not only if you have something against someone but also if you think someone has something against you.

Please practice this. There is no worse feeling than trying to lead people into worship with God and feeling tension with one of your fellow servants.

Personal holiness

Then there is the issue of personal holiness. The apostle Paul's admonition is applicable to every age in every age. In these verses he reminds us that we need to be vessels "made holy, useful to the Master and prepared to do any good work" (2 Tim. 2:20-22 [NIV]).

This is not a book on church discipline, so I want to be very careful, but there is a familial responsibility to each other in this very difficult and delicate area: "Brothers, (and Sisters) if someone is caught in a sin, you who are spiritual should restore him gently. But watch yourself, or you also may be tempted" (Gal. 6:1 [NIV]). If a problem along these lines arises seek the immediate help of your pastor.

Private Worship

An old adage that is very much at work here is this, "You can't lead people to a place you haven't been or are not willing to go yourself" or as a college choir director once put it, "You can't give the audience goose bumps if you don't have them first."

So, how well do you know the God you are worshiping? How's your relationship? If the praise band is going to lead people into God's presence, has the praise band been there first?

Musical styles come and go—this remains constant. When I read King David's songs I'm not sure what musical style he wrote them in, but I do know the Spirit he sung them in. It's the same Holy Spirit that empowers us today. You want to be sure that it's the Spirit that's there on the chancel with you on Sunday.

However, to have that Spirit with you on Sunday in front of the people, you need to have it with you during the week when it's you in prayer. If you don't, the remedy is simple: *ask*, *seek*, and *knock* as Jesus tells us in the Sermon on the Mount. In that passage, Jesus says that God will give "good gifts"—and we know there is none greater than the gift of Jesus.

It can't be stressed enough that all members of the praise team need to be able to worship alone before worshiping before the crowd.

General Suggestions

Especially for music leaders and directors, here are general guidelines that we try to go by at The Church of the Resurrection.

1. Pray with the team before and/or after rehearsal and service (any opportunity).
2. Identify and celebrate those times when you felt worship happen and you were aware of the presence of God.
3. Enter into worship expecting those times to happen.
4. Always be in the process of studying scripture and/or books about worship.
5. Take the spiritual not just musical lead.
6. Do a retreat with the band if possible.
7. Give an opportunity for people to get to know one another and for each person to pray. Have members share how they came to faith.
8. As leader, give yourself to private worship. If you are not entering God's presence in your prayer closet, you will not lead people there in public. (Sometimes I worship by putting on my favorite Christian music. I will sing at the top of my lungs and dance with all my might. I am swept away by the sheer joy of the good news of Christ and all it means.)

Finally—Making Disciples

People are busy. Music is a service ministry where you serve by preparing others to serve the congregation. If you are like me, even if you were to set the spiritual part of that preparation aside, just the mechanical aspects of getting your team musically ready takes more time than you really have. However, discipleship is not a suggestion, it is our Lord's "Great Commission."

So, work on the music—there's nothing wrong with that, but do not neglect the much, much, much weightier matter of the soul.